Happy
Valentine's Day
to:

To My Valentine's Day SweetHEART

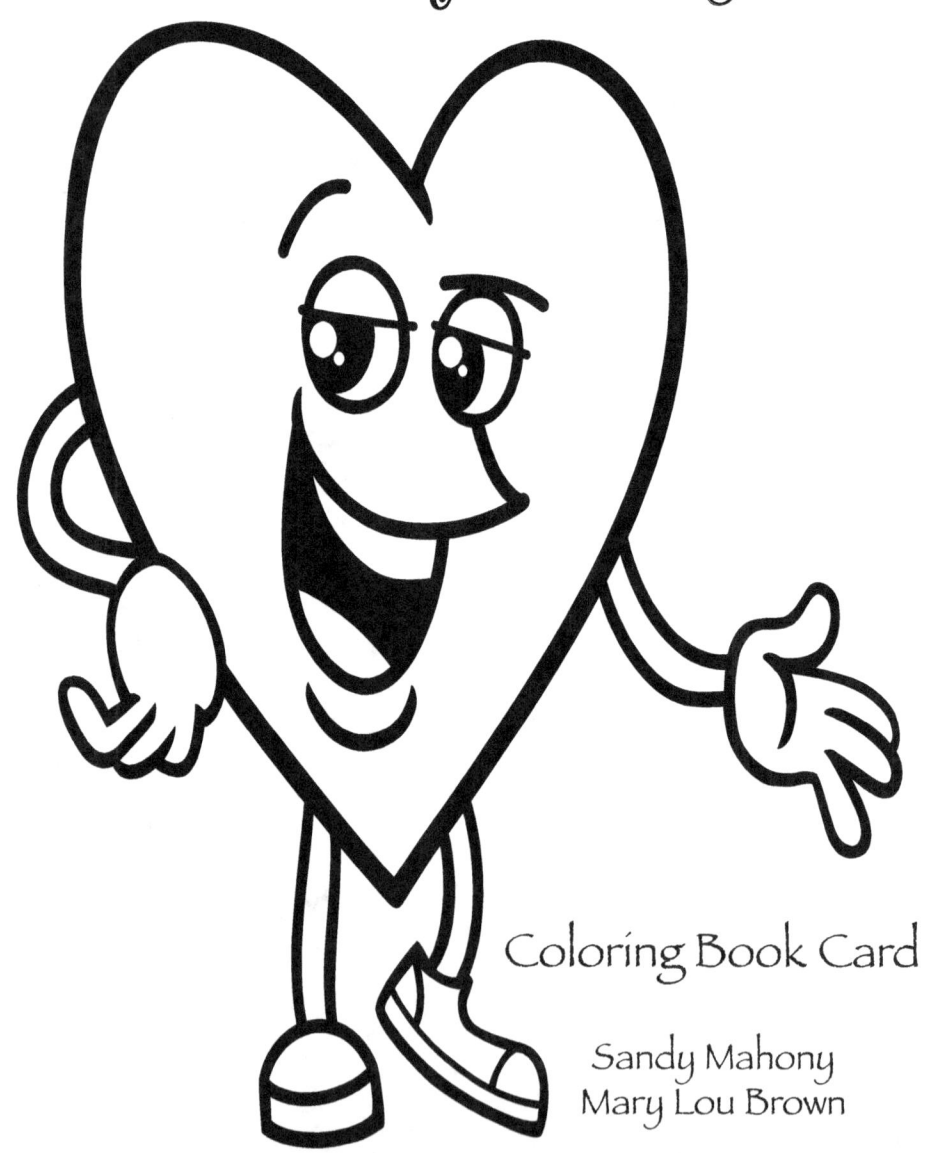

Coloring Book Card

Sandy Mahony
Mary Lou Brown

you had me at Hello

All you need is Love

I miss you

my heart is where you are

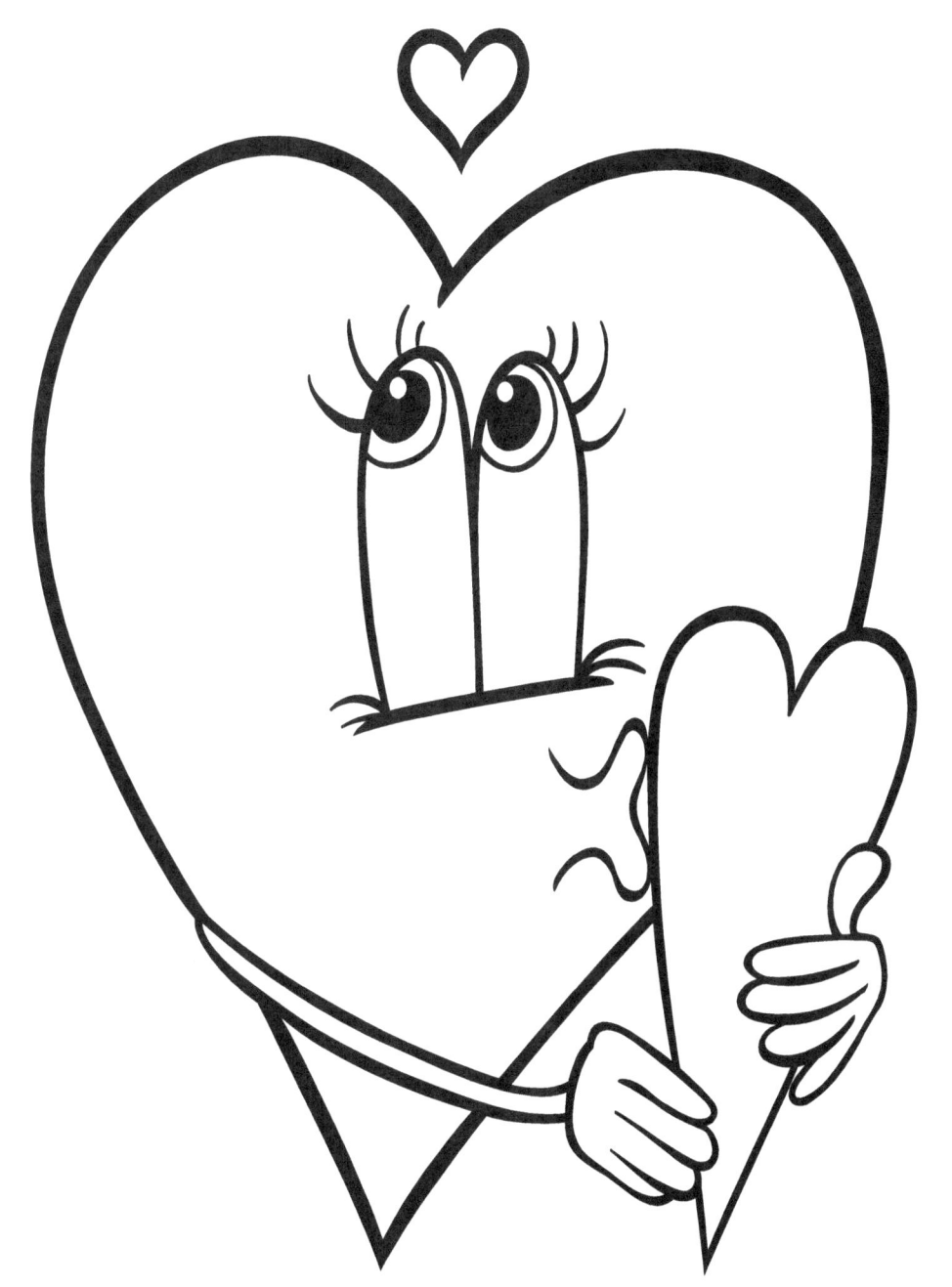

a true LOVE StoRy never ends

love is in the air

You make my heart smile

our love is Magic

THE
STARS
They SHINE
FOR YOU

All of me LOVES all of you

one love one heart

P. S.
i love you